The Pious Undertaking Progresses:

the Chantry Chapel of St Mary the Virgin, Wakefield Bridge, in the nineteenth, twentieth, and early twenty-first centuries

by

Kate Taylor

Wakefield Historical Publications

WHP 44

First published in 2011 by
Wakefield Historical Publications
a body comprising Wakefield Historical Society
and the City of Wakefield Metropolitan District Council,
formed in 1977 to publish monographs on topics
of regional significance.

All rights reserved

ISBN 978-0-901869-47-0

Wakefield Historical Publications
19 Pinder's Grove
Wakefield
West Yorkshire
WF1 4AH
Tel 01924 372748

Printed by Cerberus Printing
www.cerberusprinting.co.uk

Introduction

Was the restoration of Wakefield's bridge Chantry in the 1840s a sublime act of faith or an act of folly?

This was the question posed in *This Pious Undertaking* which provided the first detailed account of the background to that restoration and of the subsequent chequered history of the chapel.

The present book is little more than a revision of the original history although it updates the story by almost a further decade.

The introduction to *This Pious Undertaking,* with its comments on the 'faith or folly' issue is reproduced here.

'On the one hand we have a house of prayer, rescued from three hundred years of secular use and restored as a place of worship where still today, more than 150 years after the restoration, services are held regularly. Then, too, the Chantry is one of only a handful of (partially) surviving medieval bridge chapels in England. It is also a significant local landmark. It holds a place in the hearts of local people. On open days it can draw well over a hundred visitors.

'On the other hand the restoration meant the replacement of most of the medieval building with a Victorian one and in stone of such poor quality that it has needed frequent and costly repair. Although the restoration scheme was initiated by the Vicar of Wakefield, the creation of a new ecclesiastical district in 1844 meant that the revived chapel became, virtually accidentally, the responsibility of the always impoverished parish of St Mary. Later, when slum clearance led to a merger in 1966, it was left to the people of the amalgamated parish of St Andrew and St Mary to maintain both the fabric and the services. This proved a heavy – and surely unfair – burden on a comparatively poor parish with other churches in its care.

'Such were the difficulties faced by St Andrew's that in 1990 a body of Friends was formed to raise funds for the repair and maintenance of the building. This eased the financial problems but the Vicar of St Andrews remained responsible for the acts of worship.

'At the beginning of the new millennium, however, with a neat re-drawing of parish boundaries, the Chantry has been returned to the parish of Wakefield and it is with the Dean and Chapter of Wakefield Cathedral, the former parish church, that its future rests.'

The first years of the 21 century have seen developments in the area of the Wakefield waterfront that have provided a new setting for the Chantry which today seems less 'out on a limb' and more at the heart of a growing community. Importantly, the opening of the Hepworth Wakefield in May 2011 has provided with chapel with a neighbour that seems likely to draw very many tourists both to the gallery and to the bridge chapel. Whilst the chapel itself has been used increasingly for worship, it has also seen a growth in use for cultural events and for education. Perhaps we need no longer regard its rescue in the 1840s as an 'act of folly' but as an act of faith which is now well rewarded.

The Chantry painted by J M W Turner in 1797 C Trustees of the British Museum

The Pious Undertaking Progresses

The earlier history

The Chantry Chapel of St Mary the Virgin, buttressing Wakefield Bridge, was reopened for worship on Easter Sunday, 22 April 1848 after some 300 years in secular hands. The prime mover in bringing about the restoration was Samuel Sharp (1773-1885) who had been the vicar of Wakefield since 1810 and in whose large parish the Chantry lay.

The earlier history of the Chantry has been fully told elsewhere; a brief summary is all that is needed now.[1] It was one of four such free-standing medieval chapels erected beside each of the main routes into Wakefield and it was built in the mid fourteenth century by the townsmen of Wakefield as an integral part of their new stone bridge across the River Calder. It was licensed in 1356 and was served, normally, by two priests whose task was to say masses for souls supposedly in purgatory. Following the Dissolution of the Chantries in the sixteenth century it passed through various hands until being given in the mid seventeenth century to the Trustees of the Wakefield Poor. In response to questions from his archbishop in 1764 the Vicar of Wakefield referred to the 'chapel upon Wakefield bridge...in which no divine service has been performed time out of mind.[2] In 1797 it was leased to the West Riding magistrates, who were responsible for the maintenance of the bridge. At various times it was used as a warehouse, an old clothes shop, a 'den' for flax dressers, a newsroom, a cheese-cake shop, a reservoir to supply the town with water by carts, a hospital for soldiers and a prison to flog them in, a shop for woolcombers, premises for a tailor, and offices for a corn merchant at a time when Wakefield was a major inland port. A fireplace had been installed at some point and the roof pierced by a chimney. The spiral staircase in the north-east corner, leading from the crypt to the turret, had been used in part as a coal store. Interior features such as cornices and the canopy had been hacked away but it seems that, even in the 1840s, there were traces of medieval frescoes. There had been repairs at various periods. In the early nineteenth century, the fine tracery of the windows had been replaced by cross-headed mullions and eighteenth-century sash squares. In 1798 four short pillars had been inserted into the finely-sculpted front to strengthen it.[3]

The re-building of the 1840s

Demands for the restoration of the Chantry sprang from a blend of antiquarianism and a renewed interest, brought about by the Oxford Movement, in the perceived beauties and rituals of the medieval church. From the late eighteenth century the chapel was increasingly revalued, portrayed by artists, including J M W Turner who painted it during his 1797 tour of Yorkshire, or noted by travellers and antiquaries. In 1806 and 1809 it was the focus of articles in *The Gentleman's Magazine*. There was a report in 1824 that Wakefield's Roman Catholics might seek to acquire the Chantry but this came to nothing and the purpose-built St Austin's, in Wentworth Terrace, was opened in 1828.[4] Then, again in 1828, the Morley antiquary Norrisson Scatcherd (1780-1853) published *A Dissertation on Ancient Bridges and Bridge Chapels especially that remarkable edifice on Wakefield Bridge*. Ten years later a number of letters appeared in the local newspaper, *The Wakefield Journal*, calling for the restoration of this 'splendid example of English taste and English piety', this 'exquisite relic' after years of 'desecration, decay and miserable defacing'.[5] The area close to the Chantry was by this period densely populated, largely by the working-class associated particularly with the mills and warehouses by the river, or with the boats themselves. One writer drew attention to the urgent need for church accommodation 'in the very centre of our whole river population'.

But nothing was done.

Then on 26 July 1842 the Yorkshire Architectural Society was founded at a meeting in Leeds presided over by Walter Farquhar Hook (1798-1875), the Vicar of Leeds. This step was inspired by the Oxford Movement and, as its foundation resolutions make clear, was conceived as a sister body to the Oxford Architectural Society, the Cambridge Camden Society, the Exeter and Lichfield Diocesan Societies for Promoting the Study of Ecclesiastical Architecture, and the Durham Architectural Society. Its objects were 'to promote the study of ecclesiastical architecture, antiquities and design, the restoration of mutilated architectural remains, and of churches or parts of churches which may have been desecrated, within the County of York, and to improve, as far as may be within its province, the character of ecclesiastical edifices to be erected in the future.'[6]

Samuel Sharp was among the first to join the Society. What better 'mutilated architectural remains' to restore than the Chantry on Wakefield Bridge? Sharp was one of the Trustees of the Wakefield Poor, the body in which the freehold of the chapel was vested. He seems to have had little difficulty in persuading his fellow trustees to return the building to the Church. On 10 October 1842 Sharp applied successfully to the West Riding magistrates to relinquish their lease of the building, for which they were then paying a shilling a year, and to give their tenant notice to quit.[7] He reported his success a month later to the Yorkshire Architectural Society and asked it to undertake the task of restoration.[8] He opened an account for donations towards the work and wrote in November 1842 to the Ecclesiastical Commissioners to say that he believed the Trustees of the Wakefield Poor would give the Chantry free, provided that it was set apart for worship, and to enquire whether the Board of Commissioners for Building Additional Churches would be willing to accept the gift. He would himself pay the legal expenses.[9] In February 1843 the Chantry was conveyed 'freely and voluntarily and without any valuable consideration' to Her Majesty's Commissioners for Building New Churches.[10]

Norrisson Scatcherd, still closely interested in the fate of the chapel, appealed via the press to 'Antiquaries and Odd Fellows of all kinds, whether Brethren of the Masons or of the secret order of the Peaceful Dove, whether Whigs or Tories, churchmen or dissenters', to throw their 'mite' into Sharp's 'treasury'.[11]

Designs for the work were the subject of a competition promoted by the Yorkshire Architectural Society. Eight schemes were submitted anonymously and in March 1843 a sub-committee of the Society chose that of George Gilbert Scott (1811-1878).[12] Scott, later to become one of the greatest exponents of Victorian gothic architecture, had already designed the Martyrs' Memorial in Oxford and a major restoration of Chesterfield parish church. He had been 'converted' to high church ideas by Benjamin Webb (1819-1885), the secretary of the Camden Society, and by the writings of Augustus Welby Northmore Pugin (1812-1852).[13] Amongst other competitors were the father and son John Chessell and Charles Buckler. Scott's scheme for the Chantry was estimated as costing £2,500. The Yorkshire Architectural Society, resolving that it must 'rally to assist this pious undertaking', set up a second sub-committee to assist Sharp with fund raising and voted £30 from its own resources to the cause.[14]

Meanwhile a quite different development was taking place which was to affect the future of the Chantry. The apparent lack of religious belief (or at least religious practice) amongst the urban poor was a perennial Victorian concern. In the 1840s the view seemed to prevail that the absence from worship might be due to the shortage of available seats in the existing churches where indeed often many of the pews were privately owned or tenanted. There was also some very real concern at the possibility of anti-Establishment activities, in particular via Chartism. Thus proposals to extend the influence of the Church of England reflected the need to maintain a more deferential and respectable, God-fearing, even minister and bishop-fearing public. Religious and moral teaching, provided by the churches through their National schools, were regarded as the means of forestalling trouble. Lord Ashley, campaigning to provide additional funds for the National schools themselves, argued in Parliament that principles of religion and respectability must be taught as a matter of urgency to counter the 'terrible wilderness of spiritual devastation and the surge of juvenile crime and of drunkenness' (over 11% of all crime in 1842 had been committed by juveniles and the crime rate as a whole was rising).[15] All this resulted in the Church Extension Act of 1843 'to make better provision for the spiritual care of populous parishes' – in other words to ensure that religious teaching and pastoral care were brought to the urban working classes. The Act, which followed similar ones, allowed for the creation of new ecclesiastical districts, provided that the diocesan bishop approved, and provided that the incumbent of the parish which was to be divided had seen a draft scheme and had the opportunity to comment. The minister of the new district would be granted not less than £100 a year to be increased to £150 once a church had been built and consecrated and the district had become a new parish. Compensation would be given to the incumbent of the original parish which was losing a part of its patch. The gift of the living would for the time being rest with the bishop and the crown, each nominating a minister in turn. But if a patron were to be found (and this provision became important later) who was prepared to contribute to a permanent endowment for the living, then the right of patronage could be appropriately assigned elsewhere.

The Church Extension Bill gained the support of members of Parliament of both Tractarian (Oxford Movement) and evangelical sympathies. Although each side was concerned with the sort of ministers who might be appointed, almost all agreed that some ministers of some sort of churchmanship were essential. Interestingly, for the same fundamental issues are perennial, at least one MP argued that public order would be better maintained by improving people's living conditions than by giving them more churches.[16]

The 1843 Act was an enabling measure. In 1844, in accordance with its provisions, an Order in Council was made authorising the creation in the south-eastern part of Wakefield of two new and neighbouring, largely working-class ecclesiastical districts – those of St Andrew and St Mary, the latter including the Chantry within its bounds. Both came into being on 3 September 1844. Thomas Brown Parkinson, a keen Puseyite, was appointed as the incumbent of St Mary's in December and a room above a stable near to Kirkgate Station was converted into a chapel and schoolroom.[17]

In addition to his Sunday services, Parkinson, who lived in Ingwell Street and later in Kirkgate,[18] conducted services every morning at 7.30am, offered prayers and sermons on the eve of religious festivals and saints days, and held a service every Wednesday and Friday evening in Lent. He established a system of district visiting and founded a lending library based on the schoolroom cum chapel.

Progress on the Chantry scheme, still masterminded by Sharp, was slow, largely, it must be assumed, because of the difficulty in attracting the necessary finance, and it seems to have been only in the summer of 1847 that work began.[19] Scott's scheme, much to his later regret, was more of a rebuilding than a restoration. It involved taking down all that remained of the chapel above the crypt. The original front was removed and bought by the Hon G C Norton to be taken to the grounds of Kettlethorpe Hall where it provided the front of a boathouse until vandals wrecked it in the early 1990s. An inscription, now lost and not entirely accurate, read

This sanctuary is constructed with the remains of the original West Front and other fragments of St Marie's Chantry which was built on Wakefield Bridge in the reign of Edward III about 1357.

It was restored after the Battle of Wakefield fought AD1460 – but defaced by repairs done by the County AD 1794.

In the restoration of AD 1847. the ruins of the Chantry were purchased by the Honourable George Chapple Norton and re-erected in the same year by him on this spot under the supervision of William Cox Sculptor[20]

The statue of the Virgin Mary which was placed on the outside of the chapel in 1848 in a niche above the east window. Photo by Brian Holding

New stone from Bath and Caen was bought for its replacement. The stone for the other walls is said to have come from 'near Milford'.[21]

Although Scott aimed to reproduce the chapel as it must once have been, the theological tensions of the time precluded anything that smacked overmuch of Mariolatry. Above the three doors of the original west front was a frieze of five rectangular panels. The first four depicted the Annunciation, the Nativity, the Resurrection and the Ascension. The fifth it was thought portrayed the Coronation of the Blessed Virgin. In Scott's design this was replaced by an 'imaginary representation' of Mary and Jesus in Heaven.[22]

Only two of the six niches on the front of the chapel were provided with figures. At the apex of the east window, on the outside of the chapel and facing down the river, a further niche was filled with a statue of the Virgin. An interior niche in the east wall, to the right of the altar, assumed to have held a similar statue, was recreated albeit without any figure, and Scott made use of some of the surviving stone for its elaborate canopy. His drawing for this, now in the RIBA drawings collection, seems to be the only design of the scheme to have survived. The niche now holds the statue that stood in 1848 above the east window. It was brought inside after falling into the river.

Stained glass by Barnett of York was placed in the great east window and in the most easterly of the three windows on either side wall. The middle window on the south side was provided with glass by Wailes of Newcastle soon after the building was opened for worship but the remaining three windows had, and still have, plain glass panes leaded in a diamond pattern. New stone heads, depicting Edward III (1312-1377) who was on the throne when the chapel was first built, and his queen, Philippa, were provided as label stops on either side of the east window. No information has been found about the heads beside the side windows. Two richly carved crossbeams, one bearing the legend in Latin, 'The Word was made flesh, Glory be to God', supported the roof and the ceiling was panelled in oak. A bell from the local foundry of Blackburn and Teal, in F sharp, was placed in the turret. Seating was provided by the simple means of bringing the chairs across from the stable room.[23] The work finally cost £2,200 of which by November 1848 only £1,361.11s.1d had been raised. One John Maude gave £300 towards the restoration and provided an altar table. Other donations included £25 from the Queen Dowager, £105 from Daniel Gaskell of Lupset Hall, £50 from Benjamin Gaskell of Thornes House, £50 in all from the Yorkshire Architectural Society,

£27 from the Freemasons Lodge of Unanimity and £10 each from Earl Fitzwilliam and the Earl of Dartmouth. The pupils of the Proprietary School subscribed a guinea and Wakefield manufacturers Edward Green and Richard Poppleton gave £1 each.[24] Samuel Sharp later claimed that he had personally lost £200 over the enterprise and it had brought him into sequestration.[25]

The Chantry as a mini parish church

When the work (some of which was supervised by William Cox) was completed, the chapel, a mere 50 feet by 25 feet in size, originally established for mass priests of the Catholic Church, became the sole place of worship for the new St Mary's district. *The Wakefield Journal* reported the opening:

> This beautiful little temple, thus recovered to the church and most carefully restored, was opened for divine service on Easter Morning at seven o'clock. The litany was chanted by Rev C Mercer and the choir that has been formed in connection with the chapel; after which the communion office was proceeded with by the incumbent of the district, assisted by the Rev H Jones, curate of the parish church..There was a large number of communicants, a great part of whom have been brought to a sense of their duty in this respect since the formation of the district.[26]

A somewhat romanticised report in a monthly journal, *The Parish Choir*, tells us that after the Chantry was reopened, choral service was performed daily by the minister and a band of young male choristers, all robed in white.

> The effect in this tiny chapel is not one easily forgotten. It is crowded every Sunday; on the occasion of which I speak, though the rain had never abated since morning, it was filled; around us an equinoctial gale was blowing and the waters, flooded to a height far beyond their usual course, roared along as though they would sweep the little sanctuary from its foundations.

For the next eight years, the Chantry continued to serve as the church for the ecclesiastical district. Parkinson's return for the 1851 religious census shows that on Census Sunday, 20 March, there were 137 present at the morning service, 127 in the afternoon, and 106 in the evening. It had not, however, been re-consecrated. Moreover it was not licensed for marriages.

A palisade was erected in front of the building shortly after the opening to protect it from passing traffic.[27]
Less than a year after the Chantry's reopening, a site was purchased for the new church, parsonage and church school. 2,442 square yards of the Ingwell Close were obtained from Richard Munkhouse Wilson of Salisbury and conveyed to Her Majesty's Commissioners for Building New Churches.

However, Parkinson himself became disaffected with the Established Church. In 1851, leaving his district still with no church other than the Chantry, he went over to Rome, joining the Jesuit order.

Reverend Joseph Senior and the building of St Mary's

Parkinson was followed at St Mary's by Joseph Senior (1805-1897). When he became the minister there in 1851 there was not only no 'proper' parish church but there was still no parsonage house and no fit building for a day-school. 'Our only accommodation for the children is a chamber over a stable surrounded with piggeries and other nuisances,' Senior observed.[28] We must remember that elementary schooling was increasingly regarded as socially highly desirable; children of the labouring classes must be taught the principles of religion, spelling and computation, and that it was above all the Established Church that was expected to raise funds for and manage these schools. It was to providing a church, a parsonage and a school that Senior seems most diligently to have addressed himself.

Senior was a Wakefield man, attending the Grammar School as a pupil for 13 years, into the 1820s, and becoming a protégé of Dr Naylor, its headmaster. After leaving school he taught briefly at a commercial and classical day-school in Woolpacks Yard and a commercial academy in the Corn Market in Wakefield before being appointed in 1832, partly through Naylor's influence and partly by luck, to the mastership of Batley Grammar School. Luck because the trustees were equally impressed by another of the candidates and hence drew lots to make their choice between them. At the same time Senior was ordained deacon and was made priest in 1833 at York. The following year he obtained an honorary degree of Doctor of Law from Glasgow University. Senior was undoubtedly proud of this and always signed the church baptism registers with his name, followed by LL.D and the word 'incumbent'. (After he became vicar in August 1868 he signed accordingly.)

At Batley, Senior served as an assistant at the parish church. In the early 1840s and of course still Master of Batley Grammar School, Senior served as curate to Naylor at Crofton. It seems that Senior's regime at Batley was not altogether successful. However his students liked him and recalled that he taught them well. If we are to measure success by the numbers of pupils, we must see him as a failure. The school had had 60 pupils in the 1820s. By 1851 it had only twenty boys.[29] In 1844 he was chosen as the Campden lecturer attached to Wakefield parish church. Lectureships were a means whereby additional services could be provided and paid for. They had arisen particularly in the seventeenth and eighteenth centuries, the Campden lectureship being in the gift of the Mercers' Company which had established it following a legacy from Viscountess Campden.[30] Again the post was one which Senior could hold together with his schoolmastership.

On coming to St Mary's, Senior provided himself with a cottage in Warrengate at a rent of £22. 10s a year [31] and then set about putting his district to rights after that 'pervert to Rome', as he called Parkinson, had left things in rather a mess. Amongst the problems was Parkinson's decision to abandon the site already purchased for the new church, parsonage and school, and to enter into a contract to buy an alternative site for 1,200 guineas which to Senior seemed much less satisfactory, rather lower down Primrose Hill and very close to the station. One of Senior's first tasks was to extricate the District from this contract and to arrange payment of £100 to the vendor.

This was, to Senior, a quite terrible waste of money in a parish which was particularly poor and for an incumbent who was himself living, apparently, pretty well on the bread line. 'How could Parkinson be so extravagant?' Senior asks, 'And with a dissenter?' The decision to abandon the new site was taken on 20 October 1851.

In the same month Senior issued a printed appeal for funds for the new church, describing his district as embracing navigation, mills, warehouses, Station and dyeworks, and saying that the sole provision for worship was the 'beautiful chapel on the bridge' which seated only 100. 'The church is virtually closed,' he said, 'against the mass of people'.[32]

A church building committee was formed which included William Teall, the ironfounder, who lived at that time in Navigation Yard and was a director of

The parish church of St Mary's, Primrose Hill, in the 1880s. Wakefield Historical Publications

the newish Borough Market Company (hence Teall Street) and three others – Richard Dunn of Woolgreaves, F Lumb, and J W Westmorland.[33] In April 1852 Senior advertised in *The Wakefield Express* for 'Plans for a church capable of accommodating 400 adults and 220 children...the cost, including architect's commission...not to exceed £1,000.'[34] A local architect, Charles Clapham, was engaged, although the real work was done by his assistant, Matthew Ogle Tarbotton who also taught technical drawing at the Mechanics Institute.[35] Building commenced on 1 March 1853. By August 1854 the church was ready for consecration. It was, said *The Wakefield Express*, a building of 'chaste simplicity and elegance' combining 'true taste in ecclesiastical architecture' (which in the culture of the time meant that it had Gothic features) with 'moderation in expense'. It was consecrated by the Bishop of Ripon on Tuesday 29 August and was followed by a lunch in the Music Saloon in Wood Street with a cold collation prepared by the staff of the George Hotel. Richard Dunn took the chair. The Bishop referred to the 'more than ordinary difficulties' which had had to be overcome at St Mary's, by which he no doubt meant the departure of the first incumbent, and Vicar Sharp boasted of the increase in parochial districts in Wakefield during his time, and rather tactlessly urged the building of more churches and parsonages without waiting for endowments.[36] Poor Senior was, of course, still living in Warren Cottage. Moreover Holy Trinity, which had been built in 1838-9, was also still without a parsonage and was trying to raise £600.[37]

The new church was at the upper end of Charles Street on rising ground so that from the exterior the east end tended to look half buried, there being insufficient money to raise the floor much above ground level. It was in the decorated English style with a 69 feet long nave and a rather short 29 feet chancel. There were side isles of 12 feet 9 inches width, divided from the nave by arches and with a tower at the west end of the south aisle. There was a ringing chamber for a peal of eight bells but only one bell could be afforded. A spire rose another 60 feet above the tower. The windows were plain glass but a subscription list was initiated in the hope of providing stained glass later.[38]

St Mary's became a parish in its own right on 15 February 1855 when the Board of the Commissioners for New Churches approved the church itself.

The poverty of the parish

The provision of the parish church meant that the Chantry was already, after little more than six years, effectively redundant. Senior, who had preached there regularly from 1848 to 1854, held services in the chapel only intermittently from then until his leaving in 1872 (to become vicar of Horton in Ribblesdale) and not normally at all on Sundays. White's *Directory* of 1866 reports that services were held in the Chantry on Wednesday and Friday evenings. Senior, of course, had no curate and could hardly be in two places at once. His Campden lectureship meant that he took a third service on Sundays, an afternoon one, in the Wakefield parish church. Correspondence in *The Wakefield Journal* in 1856 suggested that the Chantry should be reopened for the convenience and benefit of those living on the south side of Wakefield Bridge. One writer argued that both the Campden lectureship and the evening Jane lectureship, founded in 1801, should be removed to the Chantry.[39]

The poverty of the parish is everywhere stressed both in Parkinson's time and in Senior's. The baptism register, which begins in March 1845, gives some indication of the employment of those who brought their children for baptism. (There were, of course, no marriages until St Mary's was built and licensed.) In the first years by far the greatest number (32) were described simply as labourers. On different occasions twenty were listed as watermen, nineteen were employed in the dyeworks and five in a foundry, thirteen were millers, five sawyers, seven blacksmiths, seven shoemakers, three railway porters, three inn-keepers and three bricklayers. Then there were the ones and twos of warehousemen, waggoners, stuff packers and wool sorters, an engine driver, a boat builder, a milk vendor, a hay dealer and a policeman. On fifteen occasions, a significant proportion of all baptisms, Parkinson christened the children of unmarried women.[40]

Parkinson began a clothing club with his district visitors receiving deposits each Monday in the schoolroom. Deposits were also received for those saving to pay their rents, and small bonuses were promised for every pound saved. In 1856 it was reported that the poor of the St Mary's district had been relieved through the district visitors with tickets enabling them to buy flour at a considerable reduction in price. A quantity of cotton had also been distributed.[41]

A return of 1853, when Senior was applying for a grant towards building his parsonage, shows the district as having a population of 2,289, the incumbent having the spiritual care also of the workhouse which had been erected in 1852. The district, Senior said, was inhabited almost exclusively by the lowest class, 400 of the 476 houses being rated at less than five pounds annual value. 'We abound,' he added, 'with low inns, common lodging houses and the vilest sinks of vice and iniquity'. Still without his parsonage house, Senior had to pay rent for his cottage of £22.10s a year 'which to a poor clergyman with a large family of 7 children and a sickly partner is a heavy drawback'.[42] Sittings in the new parish church had to be free; well and good since it was intended to draw in the poor and needy, but this meant that it had no potential income from pew rents. The point is stressed when Senior set about obtaining his parsonage and applied for a grant from the Ecclesiastical Commissioners' Galley Knight fund – from which, indeed, he was awarded £200. Writing to the Commissioners, Senior also stressed that the district lacked any wealthy inhabitants. However he did have one or two more affluent church members including the lawyer W H B Tomlinson (1831-1898) of Calder House, son in law of William Teall, who turned engineer and succeeded him and who served as Senior's warden in 1861. Senior actually got his parsonage in 1856 albeit at a personal cost of some £968.[43]

Church collections for 'good causes' might realise only as much as £1.17s.10d for the Society for promoting Christianity amongst the Jews (October 1855), or £1.10s.9d for the Ripon Diocesan Church Building Fund (October 1855) or a mere 13s.6d for the Society for Propagating the Gospel in Foreign Parts (December 1855), or £1.8s.3d for the Church Missionary Society (May 1856).[44]

There were better collections at the annual services on behalf of the School Building Fund, the morning and evening collections on 24 August 1856, for example, totalled £7.16s.6d. In fact the new school, to replace the room over the stable, was close to becoming a reality. Plans were approved by the Committee of the Council of Education in May 1856 and the Committee, 'admitting the extreme urgency of the case', offered an immediate grant provided that their offer was reciprocated by patrons in Wakefield. A newspaper advertisement on 30 May begged for donations in the light of the 'peculiar circumstances of this poor but populous parish'.[45]
William Teall, as chairman of the building committee, laid the foundation stone of the school on 5 August 1856 using the trowel that he had used in

1851 to lay the foundation stone of the Market Hall. The architect for the school, which cost £800, was Marriott Ogle Tarbotton.[46] By April 1857, when a soiree was held there to inaugurate it, Senior had got his new day-school building and this was opened under the mastership of I M Young on 11 May 1857.[47]

The funeral of Prince Albert, consort to Queen Victoria, was marked on 23 December 1861 by a procession and 'service at the old church'.[48] This referred to Wakefield Parish Church to which there was a grand civic procession and where the service, led by the vicar, Charles Camidge, was attended by ministers from the Nonconformist chapels (but not by the Roman Catholic priest).

It was evidently envisaged that the Chantry would be used regularly in 1862 when a new verger was appointed at St Mary's who was also 'to have full charge of the Church School and the Chantry, to keep the same perfectly clean and to attend all services and (we note the priorities) to look well to the closets belonging to the school and also to the fires of the same and the warming of the church'.[49] However there is nothing in the Church Minute Book to suggest much occurred at the Chantry between the opening of St Mary's in 1854 and the coming of a curate in October 1863 when the book records that the Chantry was opened for a service in the afternoon, Mr Washbourn, who was also the second master at the Grammar School, taking the duty.

How much was Washbourn's influence is unclear but it was during his two-year stay that the St Mary's church choir began for the first time to wear surplices and that the Vestry decided unanimously to replace the New Version of the Psalms as their hymn book with the recently published high church *Hymns Ancient and Modern* (1861) which was quite full of Tractarian hymns, the most prolific of the writers being Reverend J M Neale, founder of an order of Anglican nuns. John Bacchus Dykes, who had lived as a boy in Wakefield and who still visited the town, contributed no fewer than fifty-five hymn tunes to the book. The Vestry decreed also that the church should have a new organ, which was built by Denman of York and 'opened' on Christmas Day 1866.

Washbourn left in December 1865 but it may be that the parishioners had rather liked having the Chantry in use. The next reference to the little chapel in the Church Minute Book occurs in December 1868 when a meeting of parishioners, held at the Wakefield Arms, engaged I C Boyce as curate and set out the terms of his engagement. He was to take services in the Chantry on Sunday afternoons and Wednesday mornings; Mr Smith, the St Mary's choirmaster, was to arrange for no less than six of the choir to attend when a service was held in the Chantry and the churchwardens were to provide someone to play the harmonium there; the Chantry was to be opened first on Sunday evening 1 January 1869; it was to be advertised and pecuniary assistance was to be solicited; the offertory on Sundays was to be put towards defraying the expenses of running the Chantry. Boyce stayed less than a year but in August 1869 gave the chapel a new prayer desk before going on in September 1869 to be the chaplain at the West Riding Pauper Lunatic Asylum.[50]

After Boyce's departure the Chantry seems to have been used again only spasmodically. Another note in the Minute Book records its being reopened in December 1870 after a thorough cleaning and some alterations to the gas lighting. An amusing episode during Senior's time at St Mary's occurred in 1868 when he attempted to turn his living into a Rectory and to obtain for himself the title Rector. Charles Nettleton, who then held the Rectory Manor of Wakefield, was (and perhaps as the son of one of Senior's former pupils) prepared to sell Senior the right to the great tithes levied on the site of the church, parsonage and school. Could Senior now become Rector, he asked the Ecclesiastical Commissioners. Alas, the answer was no. The Church Tithes Amendment Act passed on 31 July 1868 ruled out the renewed use of the title Rector.[51]

Improving the school remained a concern of Senior's and in 1870, shortly after he had left the area, with his parish under the care of a curate-in-charge, G W Makinson, the foundation stone of a new Infant School building was laid by Edward Green of Heath Hall who was shortly to become Chairman of Wakefield's new School Board.[52]

In October 1871, whilst Senior remained the now-absentee incumbent small-pox broke out in the Primrose Hill area. The school log book notes a report that a black flag was being hung there and that some streets were barricaded. On October 26, following the death of one of the pupils, prayers were said both in the school and in the Chantry for the abatement of the disease.[53]

From 1872 to 1874 the incumbent of St Mary's was Amos William Pitcher.

Reverend Joseph Dunne, missions to the working classes, and the minimal use of the Chantry

When Joseph Dunne came to St Mary's as vicar in 1874, an immediate concern was to put his parish church itself in good order. It was, so it is said, in a sadly neglected and dirty state, and the unseemly gas fittings were disfiguring its beautiful pillars. New gas fittings from Jones and Wills of Birmingham were suspended from the apex of every arch at a cost of more than £50. A further £100 was spent on new heating apparatus. Carvings were executed of the heads of martyred bishops and clergy of the Reformed Church.[54]
Again the Chantry was only at the margins of the concern of the incumbent and parishioners.

Dunne had been Vicar of Gawcott and had exchanged livings with Pitcher and controversy developed as to how much Dunne should have been charged for the dilapidations at Gawcott parsonage and how much Pitcher owed Dunne for the fixtures and fittings there. The case reached the County Court when Pitcher refused to pay for the latter and Dunne consequently held out against paying for the former.[55]

In 1877 the *Post Office Directory* noted that services were held in the Chantry on Friday evenings and Sunday afternoons.

The determination to evangelise the working-classes remained strong throughout the Victorian period and both the Established Church and Nonconformists mounted mission campaigns, provided ragged churches, or held services in the open air or in popular venues. During the 1870s and 1880s there were a number of large-scale missions in Wakefield under the Church of England umbrella. Clergymen picked especially for their talent for communication, were attached, at the invitation of the host parish, to different churches in Wakefield for a ten-day campaign. In 1875 nine visiting preachers came to Wakefield for a two-week mission to convert the labouring poor. J Hollins, Vicar of St Clement's, Bristol, came to St Mary's, where the population had now grown to over 5,000. *The Wakefield Herald* observed that the programme for the St Mary's District might be regarded as one of the most important, 'owing to the fact that there exists here such vast business activity'. A mission meeting was held on the Monday morning at Edward Green's Phoenix Works in Forge Lane (ie Calder Vale Road). Green's men were joined by employees from Samuel Whitham's Calder Works and Teall and Simpson's Grease Works, all the men being given an extra half-hour's lunch break to attend. The same day there was an open-air meeting at the Kirkgate Station end of Charles Street which the town missionaries connected with the Methodist and Congregational churches also attended. A meeting on the Wednesday, on Aire and Calder Navigation premises, brought workmen employed by William Pettinger, the corn factor, Briggs and Sons at Rutland Mills, Fernandes and Co's Old Bridge Brewery, and J Oxley the blacksmith. Thursday saw a second meeting at the Phoenix works, and on Friday there was a mid-day meeting at Booth's mill, Belle Isle, which was attended by employees from Holdsworth's dyeworks. On the Sunday a mission service was held at 8am in the Chantry.[56]

One of Dunne's key concerns was to obtain a better living. In 1876 the parish was enlarged. In 1877 he was still entitled only to the £150 allowed by the Ecclesiastical Commissioners from the time the church was consecrated. Income from fees was a mere £10 a year. The population of his parish was over 6,000. Its size and poverty were such that the Church Pastoral Aid Society was then maintaining a curate. In 1879 Dunne's stipend was augmented by a further £50.[57]

There was another mission in 1881 at the end of Dunne's incumbency, when mission services were held in the Infants' School, at Booth's mill, Belle Isle dyeworks and Stubley's mill under E Brewer of St Thomas's, Islington. There is no reference on this occasion, however, to any mission service in the Chantry and one wonders whether it was perceived either as too small or simply as inappropriate.[58]

It seems clear that during the final years of Dunne's incumbency the Chantry was again unused. Moreover it was already falling into serious disrepair. A letter from the Vicar of Wakefield, then Norman Straton, appeared in *The Wakefield Herald* on 15 May 1880 referring to it as 'badly dilapidated' and in need of repairs to its roof and the broken windows. He also advocated the purchase of a stove so that it could be heated for services. In fact the deteriorating state of the Chantry had been remarked as early as 1866 when Charles Camidge noted that the stone 'has been so much affected by the atmosphere that it is being rapidly defaced and first one pinnacle and then another is yielding to its powerful influences'.[59]

Reverend Henry Griffin Parrish and major repairs to the Chantry

In 1881 Joseph Dunne, whose health was suffering, exchanged pulpits with Henry Griffin Parrish (1872-1900), Vicar of Leake, a seaside parish in Lincolnshire, from the tower of whose church, it was said, you could see the Norfolk country seat of Edward Green, Ken Hill. Parrish had been energetic in improving his church at Leake; its chancel and tower had been restored and its nave re-roofed. An additional mission church had been built. Theologically Parrish declared himself broad church and his first sermon spelled out his opposition to taking any part in sectional differences.[60]

This was unsurprising since Parrish came from strong Nonconformist stock and had himself been an Independent minister. His father was a Wesleyan lay preacher. In 1856 Parrish was admitted to the Lancashire Independent College, Manchester from which he gained a BA degree from London University. He remained at the college until 1861 when he was appointed minister of the English Congregational Church, Aberdare, an industrial community in South Wales. In August 1863 he was invited to become pastor of Potternewton Congregational Chapel, Leeds. In 1870 he began a fresh ecclesiastical career when he was ordained a deacon in the Church of England in Peterborough. He served first as a curate at Uppingham, in the former county of Rutland, and was subsequently curate-in-charge of a mission church in Northampton before moving to Leake as its incumbent in 1874. He gained a BA from Queen's College, Cambridge, in 1880 and became an MA in 1884. [61]

Parrish came to St Mary's in May 1881 and in July it was reported that, in order to reach the people at the Sandal end of his parish, he was having the Chantry on the Bridge repaired upon his own responsibility. It was said that there had been no services there for the previous three years. The roof needed attention and stained glass windows, which had been seriously damaged or broken through wanton mischief, would be replaced by plain glass until funds could be raised for their repair. The Chantry would reopen, it was promised, in August or September and services would be held on Friday evenings and Sunday afternoons.[62] In fact it was 13 October when the chapel was reopened. New gas burners had been fixed, Minton tiles had been laid at the east end and the floor on either side of the central aisle had been covered with wooden pew platforms.[63]

The Chantry in 1884. Wakefield Historical Publications

Parrish was an active figure in Wakefield church and social circles as well as in his own district where he established a mission room in a cottage in Warrengate and set out to recruit more district visitors and Sunday School teachers. We find him at meetings of the Church Missionary Society, the Church Pastoral Aid Society, presiding over a meeting of the Religious Tract Society, supporting the Wakefield branch of the Bible Society, and responding at a dinner held by the Wakefield Conservative Association to a toast to the bishop designate (William Walsham How, first bishop of the diocese of Wakefield which was established in 1888) and ministers of all denominations. Parrish applied a good deal of his energy to visiting, improving and extending St Mary's day school. New classrooms were added in 1882. The Infants and Junior School log books record his regular visits when, seemingly on each occasion, he penned a note himself recording that he had checked the registers.[64] Although strongly in favour of church schools, he was enthusiastic too about education in the wider sphere and in 1886 got himself elected to the Wakefield School Board, which had responsibility for supplementing the provision of church schools by providing secular elementary education. He was a most diligent attender and his last engagement outside the Church was at its June meeting in 1900.[65] Parrish was also associated with the Wakefield Ladies Association for the Care of Friendless Girls which had been formed in 1883 and which ran a home in George Street and an agency for providing female servants. A ready wit, he argued at one of its meetings in 1888 that he liked Wakefield because no other town gave people such ample opportunity for subscribing money. And he urged that a nation rises and falls as its women rise and fall.[66] In 1882 he served as the clerical secretary of the Wakefield Church Institution. He was also for a period a governor of the Wakefield Charities, of Clayton Hospital, and of Wakefield School of Art. Both a scholar and a theologian, he was a keen debater at the annual meetings of the Wakefield Diocesan Conference. [67]

Under Parrish St Mary's blossomed. Possibly this was due to the personality of the man himself. Possibly, too, it simply reflects the changes which had taken place in society and in church circles in the previous decades. Just to mention one 'novelty' – Harvest Festival was celebrated at St Mary's and at the Chantry for the first time and on the same day in 1870.[68] John Goodchild reports that in Wakefield the 1880s were a particularly good period for church and chapel going and that this reflects the amount of social activity provided by the religious institutions – bazaars, clubs, trips, choirs, choral societies and so on. In 1887, for example, the children of St Mary's Sunday School enjoyed a trip to Ilkley and to Bolton Abbey.[69] But it may be that Parrish was more successful than some other of the Wakefield clergy. One looks for example at the size of the collection for Hospital Sunday in 1888 when St Mary's raised £8.4s.0d to the £2.7s.10d at Christ Church. Or one looks at the collections for the Wakefield Bishopric Fund when offertories at St Mary's raised £31.3s.3d as compared with those at Christ Church of £7.3s.3d or St Michael's of £6.10s. Granted that collections at St John's raised £44.10s.10d, over £10 more than St Mary's, but then St John's was, in part, a particularly wealthy and fashionable area.

Parrish had the assistance of a curate and, indeed, for a month or two when they overlapped, of two curates.

Five years after he came to Wakefield, Parrish was improving St Mary's church. The organ and organ chamber were enlarged in 1886 and the chancel was lengthened and repaved in 1887. Stained glass memorial windows commemorated Joseph and Mary Simpson, the Scott family, Jane Anne and Elizabeth Rhodes, William Teall and Edward Teall Tomlinson and Mary Bedford Tomlinson. There was a new brass lectern. [70]

The better financial health of the parish meant that its minister could turn his mind again to the physical needs of its little bridge chapel. Already, less than forty years since its restoration, the building was in a very delicate state and the east window was 'in a ruinous condition and so insecure that it might fall out at any time' and in danger of falling into the river.[71]

Parrish obtained the services of Frederick Simpson of Westfield Grove, Wakefield, as his architect. Simpson was a Wakefield man with strong associations with St Mary's. His grandfather, Joseph Simpson, had established a bread and biscuit making business in Kirkgate which Fred's father and uncle, William and John Simpson, were to continue. Old Joseph himself had been appointed as incumbent's warden at St Mary's in August 1858, four years after the church's opening in 1854. Young Frederick had attended Enoch Harrison's Academy in Smyth Street and then served articles with Andrews and Pepper at Bradford. A churchman like his grandfather, Simpson attended Wakefield parish church, later the Cathedral. In fact he was to become the Diocesan Surveyor when the new diocese was formed. Frederick Simpson's relationship with St Mary's was strengthened at least in geographical terms when he became a councillor for Primrose Hill in 1893. He was Mayor of Wakefield in 1900 and in 1903 he became one of the original trustees of the Brotherton Charity. A freemason, he was for 62 years a member of Sincerity Lodge. Whilst he was not widely known as an architect (he seems not to have entered for any of the innumerable design competitions for anything from a Town Hall to a board school) he was the architect of the Junior School and original Science blocks at the Grammar School. But meanwhile between 1888 and 1890 he was engaged on two phases of repairs and improvements to the Chantry.

In 1888 the east window and the other three stained glass windows were restored by Powell and Son of Leeds. *The Wakefield Herald* observed when the Chantry reopened in August 1888 that, 'bearing in mind that much of the glass was injured and nearly all the lead work rotten, the result is very satisfactory'. Choir stalls were made by a Mr Squires under Fred Simpson's direction, and a new oak altar rail was provided. An organ, by A Kirkland, built specially for the Chantry and with four stops, was installed and first played on 20 May 1888 by A E Elvey to a 'crowded congregation'[72] In 1890 the Chantry was closed again for three months to allow for further restoration, in particular to the east end. The turret was virtually rebuilt. The parapets were renewed. The spire at the south-east corner was rebuilt and the walls were repointed. There is a reference to the centre canopy and the figure being 'once more' replaced. This was, of course, the figure above the east window on the outside of the building. The builder was Fred Denholme. The chapel was reopened on Thursday 6 February 1890 with Wakefield's first bishop, William Walsham How, giving the address. [73]

A storm in November 1893 did extensive damage to the already decaying front of the Chantry, dislodging large stones from each of the two pinnacles. An editorial in *The Wakefield Herald* referred to its appearance as 'pitiable in the extreme'. It noted its 'broken, defaced, and tottering walls' and described it as 'little better than an eye-sore'. A further appeal for its restoration was promised but subsequent photographs show that the pinnacles were never replaced.

Parrish seems to have been somewhat careful for his health. Wakefield Council had built its infectious diseases hospital in 1875 in fields off Park Lodge Lane.[74] This was a year in which there had been 94 deaths in Wakefield from Scarlet Fever (we forget just how fatal the disease was in the days of frailer human physique and no antibiotics). In 1896 Parrish declared that he could no longer live in his vicarage because of the proximity of the fever hospital. It was 'in the midst of a very undesirable and far from healthy neighbourhood; the smoke and stench from works in the vicinity were offensive'. Seeking help in financing a new parsonage, he claimed that he had succeeded in raising £5,000 during his incumbency to pay off church debts and improve his church and chapel.[75] He moved to Bond Street.

Renewed antiquarian interest: Battle of Wakefield services

Antiquarian interest in the Chantry was renewed in the 1890s. In October 1894 the rising young archaeologist. Dr J W Walker, gave a talk in the Church Institute on Sandal Castle where he had recently done some excavation. He had read a good many documents in tracing the history of the castle and of the Battle of Wakefield of 30 December 1460 and the Civil War siege of 1643. Walker's talk led to the somewhat romantic idea of holding a service in the Chantry to commemorate the Battle of Wakefield. (The Duke of York's second son, Edmund Earl of Rutland, had been killed in the vicinity of the Chantry.) The idea evidently found favour with Parrish. However a New Year's Eve service in 1895 brought only a meagre congregation. Parrish stressed at the time that the Chantry had no endowment, that services were held there every Sunday, and that the lighting, heating and cleaning had to be defrayed from the collections which were sometimes very small.[76]

Mrs Disney Robinson and the Peache Trustees

Until Parrish came to Wakefield, the living of St Mary's had been left under the 1843 Church Extension Act in the gift alternately of the Crown and the bishop. However, shortly after Parrish came, this was to change and the advowson (the right to appoint ministers) was bought by the widowed Mrs Disney Robinson of Torquay. She had been a Wakefield woman, Frances Rebecca Hodgson, daughter of Robert Hodgson of Haigh Hall who had in 1838 given the site upon which Holy Trinity had been built, and she had married Reverend Disney Robinson, Vicar of Woolley. Her interest in the Wakefield church scene was extended when in 1874 she endowed the living of the new parish of Christ Church, Thornes, holding the patronage herself.[77]

In 1881, Mrs Robinson's solicitor, Robert Baxter, wrote to the Ecclesiastical Commissioners offering £1,000 on her behalf for the advowson of St Mary's.

She was influenced, he said, solely by the desire to promote the best interests of the church and, once purchased, the advowson would be placed in the hands of trustees.[78] Her aim was to ensure that ministers were of evangelical churchmanship.

After a certain amount of haggling because £1,200 was asked rather than the £1,000 offered, and Mrs Robinson suggested throwing in a malt kiln which could be used as a mission room, the advowson was sold. It was to be vested in trustees of whom the Reverend Alfred Peache (1818-1900), was one (hence the Peache trustees). The value of the living was to be increased by something of the expected yield of the invested £1,200. It rose by a further £40 a year.

Alfred Peache had established a trust in 1877.[79] By 1881 it already held the advowson of Christ Church. It acquired that of St Andrew's at the same time as St Mary's and in 1889 also acquired that of St Helen's Sandal.[80] By the time of Peache's death in 1900 the Trust held the patronage of 23 livings.

Geoffrey Willett, one time Vicar of St Andrew's, quoted in *New Parishes Grown Old: St Andrew's and St Mary's* from a contemporary newspaper of the change at St Andrew's when Arthur George Whaley replaced William Bowditch as the vicar there in 1885:

During the late vicar's time the services were conducted with all the rites and ceremonies of the ritualistic part of the Church of England, but henceforth there will be a new order of things and Mr Whaley will conduct the services of his church according to the views of the evangelical party. The Hymnal Companion will be used and the new vicar will make various changes in accordance with the Trust, preaching in a black gown. Of course the cross will disappear from the superaltar as well as the candlesticks and there will be no turning to the east in the creed.'

Mrs Disney Robinson's generosity included a gift of £1,000 to St Andrew's towards a permanent endowment to provide a curate, £400 to build a new vicarage there, £300 for the church itself which resulted in the purchase of a bell, a new organ and a prayer desk, £20 towards new pews, and £10 for the day school. She gave five houses in Thornhill Street to provide homes for clergy widows. She also bought the advowsons of Holy Trinity Leicester, Holy Trinity West Bromwich, Holy Trinity with St Matthias Tulse Hill, and

Melton Mowbray church and gave £18,400 to the Church Pastoral Aid Society. She died in August 1889 in her eightieth year.[81]

Henry Parrish died on 30 July 1900. He was buried in Wakefield Cemetery.[82]

Dry rot was found in the Chantry in 1901.[83]

The proposed widening of the bridge

The question of whether or not the Chantry had been consecrated was to loom large in the 1930s. But it arose first in the early years of the twentieth century. Until this point, as far as I can discern, few outside the parish itself, apart from J Walker and the brief interest roused by his talk and essays, had, since the revival of the 1840s, taken any interest in the chapel. We find the new and very evangelical Peache Trustees' vicar, Thomas Collingwood Greenwood, telling members of the Yorkshire Archaeological Society on their visit in September 1905 that there had been a 'wretchedly meagre response' to his recent appeal for the repair of the chapel and pointing out in 1907 that the collection at services, held at 3pm every Sunday, was the only means of repairing the chapel and that it was in a bad state. Greenwood provided a little statistical data at this time. His parish had some 6,000 people living in 1,044 homes. He also had the spiritual care of people in the workhouse and workhouse infirmary. In 1903 Greenwood had written to the Ecclesiastical Commissioners seeking their help in maintaining the Chantry which was, he owned, in a very bad state of repair. 'My parish,' he said, 'is a very poor one and quite unable to meet the necessary expenses in the upkeep of this chapel which serves as a place of worship for those on the south side of Wakefield'. He added that there were services on Sunday and Thursday afternoons which were well attended.[84]

In the first few years of the century the Wakefield Borough Council reached the conclusion that the bridge over the Calder here must be widened for the passage of electric trams which first crossed the bridge in 1904, and for other increasing traffic. The medieval bridge had been widened in the past on the upstream side by the West Riding Magistrates in 1758 by nine feet and in 1797 by a further ten feet. Now the options were to widen it on the Chantry side or, again, on the upstream side where the King's Mill stood. The powerful Aire and Calder Navigation Company, owners of the King's Mill, was firmly

A view from the river bank of the 1880s showing the size of the King's Mill. Wakefield Historical Publications

opposed (it was described by the Town Clerk as 'absolutely hostile' to the scheme if it involved any tampering with the mill). Hence the plan was for the Chantry to be placed on a raft and moved downstream. The Town Clerk sought to purchase the Chantry on behalf of the Corporation. The vicar was wholly opposed to the scheme, perhaps because he saw his chapel as being taken from his care. The Bishop, Rodney Eden, thought that the Council ought not to be opposed. Hence he sought in 1901 to establish who actually owned the Chantry and whether it had been consecrated because, if not, the views of the vicar would have little legal status. Whose consent, he asked, would be necessary? Is there any record in the parish chest of the Chantry actually ever being attached to the parish of St Mary? [85]

Greenwood, the incumbent, also wrote to the Ecclesiastical Commissioners. Enquiries were afoot, he said, as to his legal tenure of the chapel which had been worked as a chapel-of-ease since 1854. The reply from the Secretary of the Commissioners was unequivocal. The freehold of the Chantry was vested in the incumbent of St Mary's.

The bridge was then under the control of the West Riding County Council as the Highways Authority and Wakefield Council applied to it in 1902 to authorise the widening. This put the Chairman of the County Council, Charles George Milnes Gaskell, in a difficult position. He was also a director of the Aire and Calder Navigation. Moreover he was clearly attached to the chapel itself. He wrote in private to the Secretary of the Society for the Preservation of Ancient Buildings, Thackeray Turner, inviting him to visit him at Thornes House and to bring the problem before the society. This resulted in a report from SPAB which concluded that the only solution was to build a new bridge.[86] The Ecclesiastical Commissioners advised the bishop to refuse his consent to the moving of the Chantry. The County Council refused to accede to the bridge widening. So, without any further widening, trams crossed the bridge in either direction, sometimes passing each other on the bridge itself, for almost thirty years.

The problem resurfaced in 1913 when Wakefield Council, in the expectation of becoming a county borough with rights itself over the bridge, again explored the widening options. Mark Potter, writing from Southgate, Wakefield, wrote to the then Secretary of SPAB, A R Powys, seeking the Society's help in protecting the Chantry, 'a hallowed place threatened by vandals'.[87] Again the plan was to extend the bridge on the east, or downstream, side to a width of sixty feet from its thirty or thirty-two feet. The borough engineer, J P Wakeford, drew up plans which included creating an extension to the island on which the Chantry stands so that, again, the chapel could be moved. Dr Walker drew up alternative plans for a curving bridge to be widened on the downstream side opposite the King's Mill but on the upstream side for the remainder of its length, thus leaving both the mill and the chapel unscathed. Concerned that the medieval bridge would be destroyed, SPAB wrote to the chairman of Wakefield bridge committee arguing that it was 'one of a few early bridges of beautiful workmanship' and that the lower part and the corbelling of the Chantry were also 'of very great beauty'. Powys reported to his committee that the Bishop 'does not want to stand in the way of any necessary improvement' but that he would be guided by the Society of Antiquaries and SPAB. The Yorkshire Archaeological Society passed a resolution 'That this Society will support any reasonable scheme by which the chapel can be preserved in its present position'. It called on Wakefield Council to give careful consideration to the plan devised by Walker. SPAB held to its earlier view that any scheme, even the demolition of the mill and the widening on the west side, would be 'makeshift'. The only real option was to build a new bridge.[88]

In fact the scheme came to nothing. Much later, when the new bridge was opened in 1933, the width of the medieval bridge ceased to be an issue.

Like Dunne, Greenwood was very concerned with the augmentation of his stipend which was, even in 1920, still only £240. In 1920, after some pleading but very well argued letters from his daughter, Katie, when her father had been seriously ill and had gone away to 'recruit' his health, a further £50 was added to the stipend. In 1921 a further £1,000 endowment was raised within Wakefield from subscriptions, a sale of work, and a grant from the Diocesan Board of Finance. The Church Commissioners matched this with another £1,000 thus adding a full £100 pa to the living. [89]

Church Army captains

Probably the most prosperous period for the revived Chantry in the twentieth century was between 1921 and 1939 when a succession of Church Army captains, attached to St Mary's, had a responsibility for the chapel. The Church Army had been founded in 1882 by Wilson Carlile, a man who had

Wakefield Bridge in about 1930. The Friends of Wakefield Chantry Chapel

accumulated a fortune of £20,000 by the time he was 25 only to see it lost in 1873 with the collapse of banking houses on both sides of the Atlantic. In 1880 Carlile was ordained, responding to the poverty he saw beyond the social boundaries of the church in Kensington, where he was a curate, by adopting a more aggressive evangelism.

A Sunday school was established at the Chantry during these Church Army days. In the mid 1930s Captain W Hutchinson attracted as many as 110 for a single service and, although the numbers varied, they were always, between then and the temporary closure of the chapel in April 1939, good.[90]

In May 1935 Captain Roberts arranged a parade followed by an entertainment on the lawn of St Mary's vicarage in aid of Chantry funds.

Calls for the removal of the railings in front of the chapel were renewed in 1929.[91] The building (at last!) of the new road bridge over the Calder in 1933 made this feasible when the medieval bridge was no longer subjected to vehicles passing each other close to the chapel front. The new bridge was formally opened on 1 June during what was regarded as Wakefield's 'year of progress'.

The restoration of the 1930s and 1940s

Interest in the Chantry Chapel from an entirely new angle arose in the 1930s. Utterly benevolent in its intention, it may inadvertently have led to no little friction and, indeed, distress. It came from a relatively new Masonic Lodge which took its name from the chapel, Chantry Lodge no 4065. The Lodge was born in March 1920. It was founded by eight Wakefield Freemasons including Roland White, a past master of Sincerity Lodge. Its founder members each received what Masons term a 'jewel' – a decorative medallion – with the Chantry pictured on it. In 1933 the members of Chantry Lodge negotiated a special service at the chapel, perhaps at the invitation of the new vicar, F T Hogarth, joining there on 18 June with members of the Chantry Preceptory of Knights Templar which had also been formed in 1920, and the Chantry Royal Arch Chapter. The service was conducted by Canon Henry Telford Hayman, Rector of Thornhill and Provincial Grand Master of Nottinghamshire Masons.[92] For some years the service became an annual event. The collection on each occasion was given to a restoration fund and could be as much as £44 on a single occasion. Services for Masons were resumed for a while after the re-opening in July 1940. Provost Noel Hopkins took the service in July 1941 and the Bishop of Liverpool, Augustus David John, in 1942. The tradition was broken for a year or two after the 1943 service but there was a service again in 1947. Services for Chantry Lodge have been revived from time to time since then and notably since the major repairs of the 1990s. Chantry Lodge has been a significant benefactor of the chapel. In 1945 at its silver jubilee it donated 100 guineas to the restoration and in 1968 it gave a further £100 to the new appeal.

It was White, or so it was said at the time, who was the prime mover in bringing about the 1930s restoration appeal. White was managing director of a warehouse concern and of Clark's Brewery as well as being for a short time chairman of the Wakefield Corn Exchange Company. At about the time of the first Masonic service, the then Bishop of Wakefield, James Seaton, began to worry about the serious state of the Chantry. Quite why is uncertain but it is worth noting that the Diocesan Registrar, W H Coles, was himself a prominent Mason and would have known White quite well. Certainly Coles appreciated the Masonic contribution to the 1930s restoration sufficiently to ask the architect, Sir Charles Nicholson, to incorporate a Masonic emblem in designs for stained glass.

Sir Charles, architect to the Wakefield Diocese as well as to the Dioceses of Chelmsford, Portsmouth and Winchester, had been nationally long renowned as a gothic specialist. Consulted by Bishop Seaton at about the time of the first Masonic service, he urged the need for immediate repair.[93]

Nicholson had been born in 1867 and his most active years as an architect had been between 1895 and 1932. He was the architect responsible for the restoration of Shrewsbury Castle and for the war memorial chapel in Rugby School. He designed St Paul's, Halifax, in 1911 and St Michael's, Castleford, in 1926. In 1927 he adapted Portsmouth parish church when it became a cathedral.[94]

The gravest problem at the Chantry was the west front which had for decades been in a far worse state than the original medieval one. Nicholson actually considered restoring the old front but reached the conclusion that it could not be taken down and rebuilt without risk of serious damage.[95] His view was supported by both Dr Walker and the owners of Kettlethorpe Hall. The alternative was to provide a new, third, front at a cost of some £4,000. The stonework of the windows would need restoration, perhaps with a form of reconstructed stone. Both north and south parapets were defective; finials had been let into slabs; the slabs had then split and the finials had fallen down. The condition of the roof and gutters was doubtful and a full inspection would be needed. The lead should be removed for this. The interior, Sir Charles thought, had decayed the worse because the building was locked for so much of the time.

In 1937, at the time when Vicar Hogarth left, or was leaving, St Mary's, the Bishop launched an appeal, nominating his suffragan, Campbell Richard Hone, Bishop of Pontefract, to chair the appeal committee. Alderman Tom Crowe, Wakefield's Mayor, promised his support. Bishop Seaton fell ill and indeed died in 1938 on the day that the Diocese was celebrating its golden jubilee. Hone was himself installed as the new bishop but meanwhile, in July 1938 he and Crowe relaunched the appeal.[96] Rowland White, who was Mayor of Wakefield in 1939, promoted the appeal aggressively.

We must note a critical new element here. The original move to restore the Chantry in the 1840s had come from within the Established Church, although its motive was primarily antiquarian. The restoration of the 1880s and 1890 was initiated by the then vicar, Henry Parrish, and the costs were absorbed by the parish itself. Even the architect had strong St Mary's connections. Now, however, the momentum came to a not insignificant extent from right outside the parish, from those who saw the chapel particularly in antiquarian and civic terms and not at all in parochial or pastoral ones. The two are not necessarily always incompatible but events were to prove that they are not always compatible either.

In February 1938 St Mary's new incumbent, the (inevitably under the Peache Trust) low church Alfred Chatfield, was inducted but he seems to have played no role in the proceedings of July or September 1938. A fund-raising garden party was planned for 7 September to held at Sandal Hall, home then of County Alderman J H Bates. In the event bad weather meant that it took place in the Council Chamber of the Town Hall, made as garden-like as possible with plants from Wakefield Parks Department and Sandal Hall grounds. A report of the function describes the platform party as including the Mayoress, Counciilor Mrs Effie Crowe, Councillor Harry Watson, the

The work of demolishing George Gilbert Scott's front in 1939. Wakefield Historical Publications

deputy Mayor and Mayoress, and Campbell Richard Hone, who was still the Bishop of Pontefract at the time but had already been elected as the new Bishop of Wakefield. There was no mention of Alfred Chatfield. The bishop spoke of the Chantry as a great treasure, which belonged to Wakefield as a whole and announced that when it was restored it would be available for use for prayer, quiet and meditation.[97]

Correspondence of the time suggests that the effect on Vicar Chatfield was dramatic. The Bishop proposed that, after its restoration, he would grant a licence to the vicar for the use of the building. Chatfield immediately insisted that no licence was required; as the incumbent of the parish in which it lay, he had clear rights in the Chantry and neither he nor the Peache Trustees would part with them. He, and not the bishop, would determine the Chantry's use. This raised a whole new can of worms at the centre of which was the question again of the actual status of the Chantry, whether it had been licensed, or even consecrated. The bishop thought it best regarded as an unconsecrated mission church or as a chapel of ease but urged that the issue should not be raised in committee. He wrote a heated letter to Chatfield arguing that since large sums of money had been raised by both church people and the general public for the restoration, it was only right that the Bishop should have some say in its use. The problem was somewhat further complicated by the fact that, if the building were held to be consecrated, a faculty would be needed for the restoration work. Hone decided that it should be regarded as unconsecrated. However, when his opinion was sought, the secretary to the Ecclesiastical Commissioners insisted that the building must be regarded as consecrated and hence properly lying within Chatfield's control. 'There seems nothing to be done to transfer the chapel from the priest incumbent,' he wrote, 'unless the (Diocesan) Chancellor were to decided that he had power to place the chapel under the control of suitable trustees'. Then he came up with the most remarkable suggestion – why not get the boundaries of St Mary's parish changed and arrange for the Chantry to lie within the parish of Christ Church'.[97]

The new west front, designed by Sir Charles Nicholson, and based on drawings of the Chantry and on the remains of the medieval front, was built using stone from Darley Dale, and dedicated in July 1940 although a faculty was granted, at the request of the Archdeacon of Pontefract, only in January 1948.[98] The chapel was reopened. The Parochial Church Council purchased 24 new chairs and the oak chest which stands at the back of the chapel today and which was provided for donations for the chapel's upkeep.

By now war had taken over and further work was delayed.

After the reopening of the Chantry in 1940, an increasing burden was placed on the parish when the Bishop requested that the chapel should be open every day and a caretaker, a Mr Mitchell, had to be appointed.

Alfred Chatfield left St Mary's in 1945; ironically he had been responsible for services at Christ Church as well as at St Mary's and the Chantry for the last three years of his stay. His successor, John Alexander Macdonald, was inducted in the following year. Like Chatfield he was strongly evangelical in the Disney Robinson tradition.

Now further difficulties arose. Miss Edith Carlill, who died in Scarborough in February 1945, left £2,250.19s.9d (or half her estate) for the maintenance of the Chantry. Despite the 100 years or so in which incumbents of St Mary's had accepted responsibility for the Chantry, the Diocesan Registrar advised the vicar that he rather thought that, 'in view of the character of the building, etc., the Bishop of Wakefield may well feel that it would be well for you to send the bills which might be paid out of this fund to me'. At the same time Coles wrote to the Diocesan Chancellor commenting that 'You will understand that the PCC is not a body which might be entrusted with the repair of a building of such importance as if it were merely a mission church'.[99]

Macdonald was enthusiastic about the Chantry. Indeed in 1946 he wrote to Bishop Hone, 'I have fallen in love with the Chantry...I intend to do my utmost to help visitors to enjoy the beauty of our chapel.' [100] He wanted to increase the number of services again and to reopen it on weekdays to visitors. In February 1947 he set out his plans: there would be communion on the first Sunday of the month after evening prayer and on the third Sunday at 8am. Evening prayer would be conducted each Sunday at 6.30pm. At 2.30pm each Sunday there would be a children's service in the chapel and a Bible class for adults in the crypt. Macdonald hoped also to hold mid-week services for adults and for children. 'These services in the Chantry,' he declared, 'are essential to the work of ministry to people living in that part of the parish beyond the Chantry.'[101]

Additional friction focused in particular on the continuing restoration. In their enthusiasm for historical accuracy, the Restoration Committee had fully accepted Sir Charles Nicholson's plans. He had proposed to reinstate the Chantry as a medieval building and, in proper antiquarian manner, he had studied the evidence of paintings and engravings that pre-dated the 1848 rebuild, not, apparently, questioning their accuracy. The new west front must have near life-size statues in the various niches. These had been sculpted before the war but had languished in store and remained unpaid for. Money from the appeal fund had been exhausted despite generous donations from the Freemasons. Coles wanted to finance them from the Carlill bequest. Not only did the St Mary's PCC oppose this, they were also dead against having any statues at all, especially one which the Registrar spoke of as the BVM. Macdonald asked for PCC representation on the Restoration Committee. And the PCC argued that statues had been removed generally at the Reformation; they were an offence to Christians and led to idolatrous worship, the second commandment forbade them, the Carlill money was needed for rather more essential work.[102]

Now the question of consecration became significant again. If the Chantry were held to be consecrated, all work done on it would be carried out under a faculty issued by the Diocesan Chancellor. The St Mary's PCC would have to apply for faculties for whatever they chose to do to the building and a faculty would be need for the placing of the statues. Perhaps once a faculty had been granted, the erection of the statues would be almost mandatory. Faculties were applied for, not in the customary way by the vicar and churchwardens, but by Coles with the explanation that, since the restoration was done by the Archdeacon's committee it had been thought better to submit the application that way. Thus it was in 1948 that a faculty was sought for the erection of the new front that had taken place in 1940. A faculty for fixing six statues in the six niches 'to replace those that were there originally' was granted on 20 May 1948 to the Archdeacon of Pontefract.[103] The statues were put in position in the same year.

In the 1950s, care of the Chantry was squarely back in the hands of the vicar, John Macdonald, and the Parochial Church Council and its reports focus on the high cost of stonemasons' work in repairing the windows. Death watch beetle had ravaged the roof and the floor between the chapel and the crypt. In

November 1952 it was reported that the sum left under the Carlill bequest was almost exhausted.[104] By 1953 it was able to report that the urgent work of repairing the roof had been consolidated but that an appeal would be necessary if any further work was to be done. For a time in 1954 the chapel was closed while the tiles in the centre of the floor were replaced by stone flags and the east beam was renewed.[105]

In the late 1950s and early 1960s, and apparently in part because of a belief that the Chantry would be taken out of its hands, the PCC did little further to maintain the building.

For a time in the 1960s the crypt of the Chantry was used by the Rover Scouts, under their district leader Eric Dawson, for investitures. The crypt was regarded as serving an ecumenical purpose.[106]

The closure of St Mary's

It would be fair to say that St Mary's had been doomed for many years when the majority of properties in the parish were demolished under slum clearance orders. When Bishop Ramsbotham suspended the patronage of St Mary's in 1960 to facilitate its closure, and gave its care to the Vicar of St Andrew's to hold in plurality, George Clarkson, the then Bishop of Pontefract, warned him of the 'a very tough fundamentalist-revivalist-interdenominationalist core' at St Mary's who would oppose any move to make the church redundant.[107] The fate of the Chantry was an attendant issue. Clarkson's successor as Bishop of Pontefract, Eric Treacy, suggested in 1961 that the boundaries of St Catherine's and St Mary's parishes might be altered to leave the Chantry and the bridge outside either of them. The Chantry would then be extra parochial and treated as a 'peculiar'. It would have its own management vested in a committee under the Bishop.[108]

St Mary's Parochial Church Council campaigned vigorously against the proposal for the union with St Andrew's. It was, they said, 'the only church in the district with a strictly conservative evangelical tradition' which brought people from many parts of Wakefield to worship there.[109] In October 1963 the bishop wrote that there were two choices before them: the better option was to eliminate the parish, pull down the church, sell the vicarage and let St Andrew's absorb it; less good was the possibility of unscrambling the plurality and requiring St Mary's to find the money for its upkeep. It would, he said,

be 'a retrograde step..it encourages a sectarian mind in a small group of supporters'.[110] It was more important, he felt, to set free both money and men to serve the Church overseas. The Peache Trustees, patrons of both St Andrew's and St Mary's could find no one who would accept the living. The church closed on Easter Sunday 1964 but for some time remained standing, a prey to vandals and a constant anxiety to the Vicar of St Andrew's who pressed for its demolition.
No steps were taken to resolve the question of the Chantry.

In the event, St Mary's was united with St Andrew's in 1966 and, reluctantly, the vicar and PCC of St Andrew's found themselves responsible for the bridge chapel. St Mary's itself was demolished and the materials and site disposed of. Under the Reorganization Measure a half of the proceeds from any sale was to be applied to the work of the repair of the Chantry.[111]

That money had to be chased up later during the 1967 appeal.

The 1967 Appeal

A meeting in the Town Hall in November 1966, initiated by the Chantry Lodge of Freemasons and Bishop John Ramsbotham, heard a report by the York-based architect, George Pace, on the urgent repairs that were again needed to the Chantry. The south-east corner was in danger of collapse, the east wall needed to be stabilised and the stonework of the east window to be renewed.[112]
This time an application for a faculty for the repair work was put forward by the new incumbent of St Andrew's, Reverend Geoffrey Thomas Willett, and his churchwardens, but they added to the application form the observation that there was difficulty in attracting more than 15 worshippers, the continued maintenance of the building depended solely on the invested £180 which remained from Edith Carlill's bequest and that the Chantry suffered from the vandalism prevalent in this part of the town. [113]

An appeal for funding came in April 1967 when £15,000 was sought from a public which was comparatively unresponsive despite the newish Bishop of Wakefield, Eric Treacy, sitting on the bridge on 21 June 1969 to receive donations.

By August 1968, Harold Speak, the appeal secretary, was able to report that £10,000 of the £15,000 had been raised but that shortage of craftsmen skilled enough to undertake the delicate work of restoration was delaying the start.[114] The first contract, for £7,400, for the repairs to the east wall and window only, was awarded in May 1969 to K Ferguson and Son of Ripon, but the appeal committee was advised that to complete all necessary work, including repairs to the north and south walls and windows, a total of £19,000 would now be needed.[115] The contract for work on the south side of the chapel was awarded in March 1970 despite the appeal fund still having a shortfall. Financial constraints meant that in many places where new stone was needed, the contractors had to make do with repointing and regrouting the existing worn stones. There seemed to be no question of undertaking the vital work on the north side.

The chapel was reopened after restoration work on 11 April 1971 with two of the windows on the north side boarded up. The vicar spoke beforehand of the present small congregation being unable to meet the financial needs of the building and remarked that the houses which the chapel used to serve had largely been demolished.[116]

A public meeting in the Town Hall on 3 June that year was told that more work was necessary and that a further £5,000 would be needed. An evidently frustrated Bishop Treacy remarked that 'If the Chantry chapel eventually falls into the river, it will be because the City of Wakefield has not cared enough to save it'. He also warned of the possibility of the chapel's being closed. The Church of England was at that time, he observed, concerned to reduce the number of its buildings. Mr Willett added that the Chantry was the fourth church building in his care and that financial problems were acute.[117]

Again the repair and maintenance of the Chantry was firmly back in the hands of the Parochial Church Council, this time that of the united parishes. St Andrew's PCC had been apprehensive about receiving the Chantry at all in the measure to unite the two benefices.[118] Now it seemed that their misgivings were to prove well founded. Further work on the chapel began in 1973 with the Wakefield architect Alwyn Waite and, as contractor again, K Ferguson and Son.[119]

A part of the remaining shortfall of £2,550 came in 1976 when the West Yorkshire County Council's Recreation and Arts Committee agreed to make

a grant of £1,900 towards it provided that the Chantry was opened to the public on the first Saturday of each month from April to October.[120]
Eighty wooden chairs were brought from St Mark's mission church when it closed in 1974. They had been bought in 1957 from Mealing Bros of High Wycombe.[121]

The Reverend Bryan Ellis came to the parish of St Andrew and St Mary as its vicar in 1981. In the next few years the Parochial Church Council sought unsuccessfully to negotiate the transfer of the responsibility for the bridge chapel to the Cathedral authorities. An overture in 1982 to the National Trust was also met with a rebuff. The question of the chapel's future was then referred to the Diocesan Pastoral Committee but with no greater success.[122]

In April 1983 a symposium on Aspects of Yorkshire in the fifteen century was held in the Chantry, organised by the Richard III Society, Wakefield Historical Society, and Wakefield MD Council's Library Service. Speakers included Professor Charles Ross of Bristol University, the Wakefield archivist John Goodchild, Dr Lawrence Butler of Leeds University, and Lorraine Arreed, Krupp Foundation Fellow of Harvard University.[123]

New approaches

In 1984 the Very Reverend Kenneth Unwin, then Archdeacon of Pontefract, advised Wakefield Council that the Chantry was likely to be declared redundant and sought the local authority's help in finding a viable use for the building.[124] The Planning Committee subsequently determined to recommend to the Archdeacon that an approach be made to the Redundant Churches Fund. In October 1987 there was a meeting of representatives of the Fund, the Church Commissioners, the Diocese of Wakefield, and the local authority when it was noted that the Chantry, still being used for services for a modest number of worshippers, would not be declared redundant until an appropriate new use could be found. The Diocesan authorities asked the Council to take over the building, arguing that it should not remain a financial burden on the parish of St Andrew and St Mary for any longer than necessary. This idea was given support by the local authority's Listed Buildings Panel which asked that the Council should also consider reinstating the stone sett surface of the bridge as a way of marking the 900 anniversary of Wakefield's medieval borough charter which would fall in 1990. The Planning Committee then resolved to give consideration to the twin proposals and to link these with their relevance to the Council's future policy in regard to tourism and to the development of a planning brief for the riverside area as a whole.[125] A critical meeting, convened by the Council, was held in the old courtroom of the Town Hall on 27 September 1989, with representatives of the Church Commissioners, the Diocese of Wakefield, the parish of St Andrew and St Mary, the local authority's Planning and Transport and Engineering Departments, and Wakefield's Civic and Historical Societies.[126] Alan Guthrie Jones, on behalf of the Church Commissioners, made it clear that the Redundant Churches Fund would be reluctant to take on the Chantry as its resources were already stretched; moreover, if it did, access to the chapel would be severely restricted. The Archdeacon of Pontefract argued that, having been built by the people of Wakefield, the Chantry should become the responsibility of the Council. This idea was strongly opposed by Wakefield Historical Society in view of what it regarded as the Council's poor record in relation to historic buildings. Councillor Bob Mitchell accepted that the parish 'should not be seen as a curator of antiquities'. But the idea that 'caught on' was that an independent body of Friends might be established to maintain the building. Following the meeting it was recommended by local authority officers that the Council 'have no immediate use for the building' and 'have no current package of proposals to include the chapel' although it might be included in 'the future vision for the waterfront' proposals which were 'too loose at the moment'.[127]

Public interest was evident when two open days at the chapel, organised by Wakefield Civic Society, brought more than 400 visitors.[128] After it became clear that it was unlikely that the chapel would be transferred to the Redundant Churches Fund, the possibilities of forming either a Trust or a body of Friends were canvassed at a meeting convened by the Civic Society and held in Zion United Reformed Church on 12 November 1990 at which the Diocese, St Andrew's, Churches Together in Wakefield, Wakefield Historical Society, the Chantry Lodge of Freemasons, and Wakefield MD Council were represented.[129] A steering committee was formed and working parties were set up to devise a constitution for a body of Friends, to consider publicity and activities, to look at the needs of the building itself and the concomitant finance.

The Lady St Oswald, the Right Reverend David Hope, Bishop of Wakefield, and the Right Honourable Walter Harrison, then Wakefield's Member of Parliament, agreed to become patrons of the Friends. [130]

John Gilbey (1924-2001) was elected as the chairman of the Friends with Ray Perraudin (1911-1995) as the secretary. The Friends' aims were twofold: to raise funds for the repair and maintenance of the building and to make it more widely known. The organisation was registered as a charity and an appeal was launched for £100,000. At launch of the appeal, on 8 September 1991, John Gilbey said, 'So far as we can see, the maintenance and support of cherished buildings is going to depend to a great extent upon the efforts of their owners and friends for the foreseeable future.... the Chantry embodies much of the material and spiritual character of the city ..to befriend it is a worthwhile, far-sighted and economically advantageous action. '

Huddersfield architect David Greenwood was engaged. By 1994 the Friends had effected major repairs to the roof of the chapel, including the replacement of the leading, and in 1995 the building was fully re-wired and new lighting and heating systems were installed by electrical engineer David Littlewood. As part of major repairs to the stonework, undertaken in 1996, the south side of the Chantry was provided with new stone heads as label stops, sculpted by John Schofield and portraying the Right Reverend Nigel McCullough as the Bishop of Wakefield, the Right Honourable Walter Harrison, the Lady St Oswald, Ray Perraudin, Canon Bryan Ellis, and a nameless stonemason. This phase of the work was carried out by William Anelay of York. The Friends' appeal fund was supplemented by a substantial grant from English Heritage.

Many individuals and local businesses, as well as grant-making trusts, made generous donations to the appeal. To raise futher funds the Friends organised open days, principally at public holiday weekends, and arranged talks, concerts and dramatic productions, all in the Chantry itself. In 1994 Audrey Cauldron, formerly head of drama at Bretton Hall College, performed her comedy, *Daisy's Tempest,* and in 1995 former drama teacher Arthur Starkie have his solo performance, *Uneasy lies the head*, based on the life of Charles I; this was followed in 1996 by Arthur's performance of *This son of York*, reflecting the life of Richard III. Fund-raising events were held jointly with Wakefield Girls' High School Old Girls' Association in 1998 and 1998. Garden parties were held at the home of Walter and Jane Harrison and at Bishop's Lodge. In 1993 and 1999 members of Wakefield Flower Club provided a flower festival in the chapel. What was to become a regular annual event, Christmas readings and music by the Accord Singers under their conductor Graham Sorrell, was first held in 1995. Another Friends' enterprise has been the creation of a range

The Most Reverend Dr David Hope, then Archbishop of York, at the Chantry on 4 September 2003. Photo by Kate Taylor

of picture postcards, initially just of the Chantry itself but subsequently of views of other popular Wakefield scenes.

The Friends aimed from the outset not only to return the Chantry to a state of good repair but to ensure that an endowment fund –something it had never had since the Reformation - was created to provide for its future maintenance. It was excellent news when the St Andrew's Parochial Church Council was advised in 1998 that under the will of Mrs Ruth Hepworth, a sum in the region of £44,000 had been left to 'the Guardians or Trustees for the time being' of the Chantry in the hope that it would be utilised 'for the upkeep of the fabric'. [131]

The Return to the Parish of Wakefield

As we have seen, the creation of new parishes in 1844 brought the Chantry into St Mary's parish and, when this was united with St Andrew's in 1966, into the care of the united benefice. Maintaining the services and financing repairs were never easy for either body. It had been the Vicar of Wakefield who had initiated the scheme for the revival of the Chantry in 1842. There were those who pressed strongly for the Cathedral – Wakefield parish church – to assume responsibility for it. Whilst for some years the idea was resisted, under Provost George Nairn-Briggs it became acceptable and even welcomed. A Pastoral Scheme, which involved a little redrawing of parish boundaries and was sealed on 24 November 1999, transferred the Chantry to its original parish. (The Hepworth Legacy went with it.) There was a special service in the chapel on 16 January 2000 when Canon Bryan Ellis formally handed over the keys to the chapel to George Nairn-Briggs. The Friends' constitution was amended so that representatives of the Cathedral replaced those from St Andrew's on its management committee.[132]

Under the new regime, the role of the Friends in financing repairs remained vital. The death of John Gilbey in 2001 brought changes to the committee with Kate Taylor becoming the chairman and Harry Livesey taking on the role of treasurer. The work of fund-raising continued steadily via open days and events including, in 2003, 2004 and 2005, bridge tournaments at Nostell Priory hosted by the Lord St Oswald.

The Friends' initial appeal reached its £100,000 target in 2003. The achievement was marked by a service on 4 September when the Archbishop of York, the Most Reverend David Hope, gave the address. He remained for a celebration dinner at the Cedar Court Hotel in the evening. Most of the money had already been spent and a second appeal was launched immediately for a further £100,000.

The 650 anniversary of the first licensing of the Chantry was marked by a civic service on 4 June 2006 when the address was given by Canon Jane Sinclair who had pastoral oversight of the Chantry on Rotherham Bridge. Members of churches and chapels from each of the mainstream denominations in Wakefield contributed arrangements for a flower festival on 15 July. The closure of the bridge to any through traffic meant that the anniversary could be celebrated, too, by a 'party on the bridge' with gazebos and stalls in the roadway itself.

A setback occurred in October 2007 when thieves stole the lead from the roof, at the same time breaking off three of the crenellations and some of the finials on the front parapet. The stone blocks were thrown in the river. Whilst DMW Restoration of Conisbrough were to undertake the repairs (and with steel replacing the lead), the Friends decided that all the work advised in the Quinquennial Inspection of 2007 should be carried out at the same time. Despite the contribution from the insurance company, the Friends faced a bill of some £18,000 and a considerable dent in their endowment fund. This was, however, offset to an extent by a bequest in 2007 of some £11,000 from the estate of Kenneth Woodward who died in Lytham St Anne's in 2004.

The Friends have received an annual donation from the Rowland St Oswald 1984 charitable trust and in 2009 became a beneficiary for the first time from the Charles Brotherton Trust.

It was only in 2005 that the Chantry was licensed for marriages. Such weddings as had taken place there prior to that were by special licence.

Changes in the staffing of the Cathedral brought a renewed enthusiasm for the Chantry. Increasing activities at the Chantry itself led to a focus in 2009 on the inadequacy of its facilities and the discomfort of the old chairs from St Mark's. A problem experienced regularly was of people tripping on the wooden pew platforms which had been installed in the 1880s but for which there had never been pews. The lack of a lavatory inhibited some people from attending events and brought some discomfort to Sunday worshippers and open-day stewards. Prompted by Angela Rusby, a member of the Friends who devised an ingenious scheme for providing a lavatory in the south-west corner of the building with access from the outside via the most southerly of the three existing doors, the Friends' management committee decided on a more ambitious scheme for the reordering of the chapel interior. John Bailey of Thomas Ford was appointed as the architect. The project involved removing the pew platforms, laying a new stone floor, providing 'pods' in either corner of the west end for tea-making facilities and a composting lavatory, installing new lighting and a sound system, and repairing the winding stairway to the crypt. With the advice of the Diocesan Parish Development Officer, Susan Parker, a grant of £50,000 was secured from the Heritage Lottery Fund. Further grants were made by the Alan Evans Trust, the Allchurches Trust, the Bishop's Development Fund, the Carpenters' Company, the Church and Community Fund, the Garfield Weston Foundation, the Wakefield District Community Foundation, the Manifold Trust, The Yorkshire and Clydesdale Bank, the Yorkshire Historic Churches Trust, and Wakefield Council Community Chest. Work was carried out in the summer of 2010. The main contractor was DMW Restoration.

Following the re-opening of the chapel, the service of re-dedication on 13 September 2010 was a gala occasion led by the Bishop of Wakefield, the Right Reverend Stephen Platten together with the Dean of Wakefield, the Very Reverend Jonathan Greener. It was attended by the Lord Lieutenant of West Yorkshire Dr Ingrid Roscoe, the High Sheriff of West Yorkshire, Richard Clough, the Mayor and Mayoress of Wakefield, Councillor and Mrs Tony Wallis, the Chief Constable of West Yorkshire Sir Norman Bettison, and Fiona Spiers, Head of the Lottery Fund for Yorkshire and the Humber. Dr Simon Thurley, Chief Executive of English Heritage, spoke briefly before the service, praising the 'army of volunteers' who ensure the day-to-day care of places of worship.

The chapel's medieval origins have increasingly been recognised. On 15 August 1998 the men of the 1509 Society chanted plainsong vespers there to mark the feast of the Assumption of Mary.

Interest in the association of the Chantry with the 1460 Battle of Wakefield was revived for the 550 anniversary in 2010 when Wakefield Historical Society

The exhibition by Gallery Arts held in the reordered Chantry to mark the opening of the Hepworth Wakefield in May 2011. Photo by Brian Holding

planned a nine-day 'pilgrimage' following the route taken by the funeral procession for Richard Duke of York from Pontefract to Fotheringhay in 1476. Members of the expedition visited the Chantry at the start of the 'pilgrimage' for a short talk about the role of similar chantries in the obsequies for the duke. On the anniversary of the battle itself, members of the choir of St Austin's Church and of the Latin Mass Society provided a requiem mass in the Chantry for Richard and his son, Edmund.

The Chantry has seen an increase in visits by coach parties, some of which seek an act of worship as well as a talk.

Under the terms of the grant from the Heritage Lottery Fund, an educational programme was established in early 2011 with school visits under the direction of the Cathedral Education Officer, Ali Bullivent, and with talks and short courses for adults provided on a voluntary basis. At the same time a grant for work with schools over a three-year period came from the Esme Fairbairn Foundation. Cultural innovation in Wakefield brought the bi-monthly Art Walk, with evening exhibitions at venues across the city. The Chantry became a part of this in November 2010. The most significant secular development has been the opening of the Hepworth Wakefield in May 2011 bringing a vast influx of tourists to the waterfront area. Paintings of the Chantry hang in a gallery there in a room which overlooks the chapel. To mark the opening week at the Hepworth Wakefield, the Chantry was itself open daily for an exhibition by local amateur artists under the aegis of Gallery Arts and masterminded by Brian Holding.

But the Chantry is primarily a place of worship and two further developments have underlined this. In 2011 Missa takes place there on some Saturday afternoons and monthly Julian meetings have also been held there.

NOTES

1. eg Walker, J W, *Yorkshire Archaeological Society Journal XI* (1890) p146ff, and Walker J W *Wakefield: its history and its people* (1934).
2. Annesley, C A and Hoskin, P (eds) *Archbishop Drummond's Visitation Returns, 1764 III Yorkshire S-Y,*(2001).
3. Buckler, J C and C, *Remarks upon Wayside Chapels with some observations on the Architecture and Present State of the Chantry on Wakefield Bridge* (1843), and *Gentleman's Magazine* (1806) pp 723-4 and (1809) pp 125-6, and Scatcherd, N *A Dissertation on Ancient Bridges and Bridge Chapels and especially that remarkable edifice on Wakefield Bridge:* and *The Universal British Directory, Vol IV,* (1793).
4. *The Wakefield and Halifax Journal,* 9 January 1824.
5. *The Wakefield Journal and West Riding Herald,* 11 October 1839 and 30 October 1840.
6. Printed list of resolutions at a meeting held in Leeds on the twenty-sixth of July 1842. John Goodchild Collection, Wakefield.
7. Quarter Sessions Order Book, West Yorkshire Archive Service QS 10/54 p163, Leeds, 19 October 1842.
8. Yorkshire Architectural Society minute book, 4 November1842.
9. Ecclesiastical Commissioners files ECE/7/1/20895 Church of England Record Centre.
10. Deed of conveyance dated 13 February 1843, West Yorkshire Archive Service, Wakefield.
11. *The Wakefield Journal,* 4 November 1842.
12. Yorkshire Architectural Society minute book, 9 March 1843 and 18 March 1843.
13. Article on Scott in the *Oxford Dictionary of National Biography.*
14. Yorkshire Architectural Society minute book, 8 February 1843.
15. *The Times,* 1 March.1843, p15, 6.May.1843, p16.
16. *The Times,* 6 May 1843.
17. *The Wakefield Journal* 29.November 1844 and 27.12.1844.
18. Wakefield Borough register of electors, Wakefield MDC Libraries service.
19. *The Wakefield Journal,* 9 July 1847.
20. Copy of the inscription in the John Goodchild Collection, Wakefield.
21. Banks, WS, *Walks about Wakefield* (1871), p104.
22. *The Wakefield Journal,* 28 April 1848.
    23. *Ibid.*
24. Leaflet dated November 1848, issued by Samuel Sharp, Wakefield MDC Libraries Service.

25. Letter of 10 December 1851, the John Goodchild Collection.
26. *The Wakefield Journal*, 28 April 1848.
27. Ibid, 29 December 1848.
28. Printed letter of 14 October 1851 from Joseph Senior, Ecclesiastical Commissioners file ECE/7/1/6837/1, Church of England Record Centre.
29. *Lester, DNR, The History of Batley Grammar School* (1962).
30. Walker, J W, *Wakefield: its history and its people*.
31. Form filled in by Senior on 21 March 1853, Ecclesiastical Commissioners file ECE/7/1/6837/1 Church of England Record Centre.
32. Printed appeal by Joseph Senior dated 14 October 1851, Ecclesiastical Commissioners file ECE/7/1/6837.
33. *The Wakefield Journal,* 1 September 1854.
34. *The Wakefield Express,* 10 April 1852.
35. *The Wakefield Journal,* 1 September 1854.
36. Ibid.
37. *The Wakefield Journal,* 2 November 1856.
38. Ibid, 1 September 1854.
39. Ibid, 25 April 1856 and 2 May 1856.
40. St Mary's baptism register, WDP 152/3, West Yorkshire Archive Service, Wakefield.
41. *The Wakefield Journal* 11 January 1856.
42. Ecclesiastical Commissioners file ECE/7/1/6837/1, Church of England Record Centre.
43. Ibid.
44. St Mary's Church minute book, WDP152/13, West Yorkshire Archive Service, Wakefield.
45. *The Wakefield Journal* 30 May 1856.
46. Ibid, 8 August 1856.
47. St Mary's Church minute book, WDP 152/3, West Yorkshire Archive Service, Wakefield
48. Ibid.
49. Ibid.
50. Ibid.
51. Ecclesiastical Commissioners file ECE/7/1/39246 Church of England Record Centre.
52. St Mary's Church minute book, WDP 152/3, West Yorkshire Archive Service, Wakefield.
53. St Mary's School log book, WDP 152/14, West Yorkshire Archive Service, Wakefield.

54. *The Wakefield Herald,* 26 February1881.
55. *The Wakefield Herald,* 1 January 1876.
56. *The Wakefield Herald,* 13 March 1875 and 20 March 1875.
57. Ecclesiastical Commissioners file ECE/7/1/20899 Church of England Record Centre.
58. *The Wakefield Herald,* 19 February.1881.

60. *The Wakefield Express,* 28 May 1881.
61. Obituaries, *The Wakefield Herald* and *The Wakefield Express,* 4 August 1900.
62. *The Wakefield Herald,* 2 July 1881.
63. *The Wakefield Herald,* 15 October 1881.
64. St Mary's School log books, WDP 152/14, West Yorkshire Archive Service, Wakefield.
65. Obituary, *The Wakefield Herald,* 4 August 1900.
66. *The Wakefield Herald,* 28 January 1888.
67. Obituary, *The Wakefield Herald,* 4 August 1900.
68. St Mary's Church minute book, WDP 152/13, West Yorkshire Archive Service, Wakefield.
69. St Mary's School log books, WDP 152/14, West Yorkshire Archive Service, Wakefield.
70. *Post Office Directory* 1888.
71. *The Wakefield Herald,* 10 March 1888.
72. *The Wakefield Herald,* 26 May 1888.
73. *The Wakefield Herald,* 8 February 1890.
74. Taylor, Kate, *The Making of Wakefield* 1801-1900 (2008).
75. Letter from Parrish of 21 March 1896, Ecclesiastical Commissioners file ECE/1/7/ 6837/1 Church of England Record Centre.
76. *The Wakefield Herald,* 4 January 1896
77. Taylor, Kate, op cit80. *Wakefield Herald* 31 August 1889.
78. Ecclesiastical Commissioners file ECE/7/1/6837/1 Church of England Record Centre.
79. Article on Alfred Peache, *Oxford Dictionary of National Biography.*
80. Papers of the Peache Trustees, WDP152/additional box2, West Yorkshire Archive Service, Wakefield.
81. Obituary, *The Wakefield Herald,* 31 August 1889.
82. Obituary, *The Wakefield Herald,* 4 August 1900.
83. *The Wakefield Herald* 5 and 12 January and 11 November 1901.
84 *Wakefield Herald* 23 September 1905 and 18 May 1907.

85. Ecclesiastical Commissioners file ECE/7/1/20895 Church of England Record Centre.
86. File on Wakefield Bridge and Chantry held at the headquarters of the Society for the Protection of Ancient Buildings.
87. Ibid.
88. Ibid.
89. Ecclesiastical Commissioners file ECE/7/1/20895, Church of England Record Centre.
90. Speak, Harold and Forrester, Jean, *The Chantry Chapel of St Mary on Wakefield Bridge* (1972).
91. *The Wakefield Express,* 26 January 1929.
92. Ibid, 22 June 1933.
93. *The Wakefield Express,* 6 August 1938.
94. Article on Sir Charles Nicholson, *Oxford Dictionary of National Biography.*
95. Letter of November 1937 in the Chantry file held by Diocesan Registrar.
96. *The Wakefield Express,* 6 August 1938.
97. *The Wakefield Express,* 10 September 1938.
98. Correspondence in the Chantry file held by the Diocesan Registrar
99. Ibid.
100 Ibid.
101. Letter from Macdonald to Hone, 17 July 1946, WD233/32, West Yorkshire Archive Service, Wakefield.
101. Letter from Macdonald of 28 February 1947 enclosing leaflet giving service times, in the Chantry file held by Diocesan Registrar.
102. Letter from Stella Burgess, secretary of St Mary's PCC to the Diocesan Registrar, 5 April 1948 in the Chantry file held by the Diocesan Registrar
103. File of faculties granted in the Diocese of Wakefield held by the Diocesan Registrar.
104. *The Wakefield Express,* 22 November 1952.
105. *The Wakefield Express,* 15 April 1954.
106. Oral information given to the author
107. Letter of 20 January 1960 from George Clarkson, WD233/32, West Yorkshire Archive Service,
108. Papers of the Diocesan Pastoral Committee, WD233/15 West Yorkshire Archive Service, Wakefield.
109. Ibid

110. Letter of 14 October 1963 from Bishop Ramsbotham, WD233/32 West Yorkshire Archive Service, Wakefield.
111. Order in Council published in *The London Gazette*, 2 August 1966.
112. *The Wakefield Express,* 3 December 1966.
113. Copy in the Chantry file held by the Diocesan Registrar.
114. *The Wakefield Express,* 24 August 1968.
115. *The Wakefield Express,* 5 April 1969.
116. *The Wakefield Express,* 26 February 1971.
117. *The Wakefield Express,* 11 June 1971.
118. Willett, GT, op cit.
119. Ibid.
120. *The Wakefield Express,* 12 March 1976.
121. Willett, GT, op cit.
122. Extracts from St Andrew's PCC Minutes provided by Canon Bryan Ellis.
123. *The Wakefield Express,* 4 August 1983.
124. *The Wakefield Express,* 4 September 1989.
125. Archive file, 1985-2011. St Marys Chantry Chapel, WMDC Conservation Archives, LB/A/40/183, Wakefield MDC Planning Dept.
126. Ibid.
127. Ibid.
128. Wakefield Civic Society Executive Committee minutes.
129. Ibid.
130. Newsletters and Minutes of the Management Committee of the Friends of Wakefield Chantry Chapel
131. The will of Ruth Harriet Hepworth of 30 Sandal Hall Mews, 23 July 1992.
132. *passim* Newsletters and Minutes of the Management Committee of the Friends of Wakefield Chantry Chapel.

Front cover - The Chantry in 2011. *Photo by Kate Taylor*

Back cover - The medieval front of the Chantry in the grounds of Kettlethorpe Hall in 1949. *Photo by Ron Head*